A FREE ONLINE COMMUNITY FOR BOOK LOVERS.

Founder and Creator of OnlineBookClub: Scott
Hughes
Director & Editor-in-Chief: S. Jeyran Main
Publisher: Onlinebookclub.org
Print & Distribution: IngramSpark
ISBN 978-1-988680-28-6 (Paperback)
ISBN 978-1-988680-29-3 (Digital)
onlinebookclub.org
For all inquiries, please contact:
magazine@onlinebookclub.org

Contributors

Fred G. Baker
Anthony A. Morris
J.E. Hibpshman
Michael J. Bowen
Michael O. Borthwick
N.L. Holmes
Peter S. Rush
Van Fleisher
Rob White
Jude Austin
Londyn Skye
Catherine A. Pepe
Gustavo Kinrys, MD
Alexandra Gold, M.A.
William W. Forgey, M.D.
Daniel Friedmann
Dania Sheldon
Christian Espinosa
Tony Jeton Selimi
Matthew Tysz
Franco Guazzoni
Tobin Marks
Craig W. Stanfill
Charlie Sheldon
Michael Hegarty
Russell M. Linden
Frederick J. Sievert
Mark Unger
Robert Leet
Hilary L Hunt M.D.
Noel Hankin
Phill Moser
Susan Smith Jones, PhD

TABLE OF CONTENTS

EDITOR'S NOTE

There is something special about spring that encourages everyone to look forward, set their clocks ahead, and not look back at the past season. Here we are with the third issue bringing you hope and optimism.

This issue offers raw confessions and vulnerable discussions that you will enjoy. You will realize that you aren't alone and how relatable your struggles are with your fellow writers. Let's enjoy what we have and aim for better things.

The third issue of OnlineBookClub Magazine presents discussions on writing due to abuse and making sure your voice is your own. It has confessions of authors and how to *language* your thoughts. These are topics that I know will be helpful for many authors.

For those who have worked hard to tell their stories, stayed up for hours on end re-reading and re-writing their manuscripts, and those who have looked at their work and felt lost, I want to say, dream big and be persistent.

Thank you for supporting OnlineBookClub, and I hope you enjoy the spring edition as much as I do.

Jeyran Main

Director & Editor-in-chief
OnlineBookClub Magazine

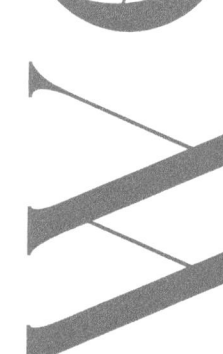

SPRING 2023 | ISSUE 03

A Letter to My Fellow Authors

Written by Anthony A. Morris

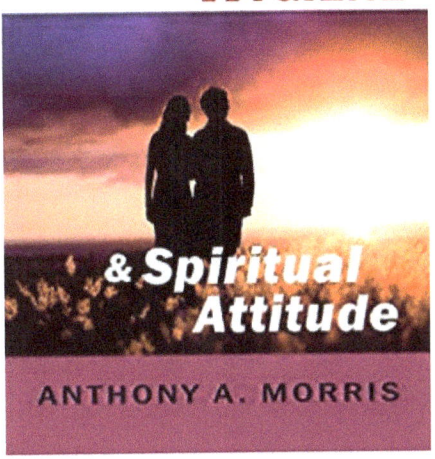

One of the many reasons I wrote the book, Good Sexual Hygiene & Spiritual Attitude, was the result of spousal abuse I witnessed as a foster parent and some situations I dealt with as an ambulance attendant.

They inspired me to write advice on certain attitudes. My experience made me understand what to look for when women get romantically involved. It allowed me to provide words of warning on how abusers act and how their wickedness will curse them in the end. Some people feel and believe it's their God-given right to be abusive. This book proves that their belief system has zero supporting merits.

My work shows why we need to develop an attitude of spending quiet time counseling ourselves on sexual respect. We need to work on our physical and mental hygiene and dedicate sincere spiritual love towards all people of our families, neighbors, and world communities.

This book exposes the Ancient Secrets that encourage hatred and provides the knowledge required to eliminate evidently detest from ourselves towards others.

I couldn't describe this book any better than what one of my reviewers said, "After reading Good Sexual Hygiene & Spiritual Attitude, readers will change the way they look at sexuality and health; in fact, they will change the way they look at and handle others."

Anthony A. Morris is the author of a Human Ethics book, Good Spiritual Hygiene & Spiritual Attitude, which was the most voted-on book of the year 2022 for Christian & Inner Peace. And the purchase-intent focus group study earned the book an incredible 30% score. The author wrote the book based on his experiences and memories from childhood, 30-plus years as a foster parent, time as an ambulance attendant, and much more. The author's belief in practicing responsible good common sense resulted in him writing this book.

Writing the Great American Novel

Written by Fred G. Baker

I haven't reached those heady heights yet, but try reading the great works of others, such as F. Scott Fitzgerald's The Beautiful and Damned. There is something comforting in the novel that contains such creative and wonderful prose. It shows me what talent can achieve even if my meager scribbling still needs to reach that level. (Not yet, anyway. I still hope to improve.)

When I attended my first writing conference, (I don't go to many—expensive, and most are directed toward novice writers. Better to save the funds for my editors.) I was awed by the authors I met who had written many books and had a strong reader following. I asked one fellow how to get started and get published. He had his own words of wisdom. He said to find the genre I wanted to work in and read the top one hundred books in that line. He said I should then pick one whose style I liked and then copy that style. That way, I would find a niche within the market.

I thanked him, but upon consideration, that was not for me. I didn't want to copy someone else. I wanted to be more creative than that.

Of course, you learn a lot by reading other authors and what worked for them in plot, style, voice, and so on. Of course, you want to learn what works in that field, but I didn't want to be a copycat. How could I be creative if so constrained?

My words of wisdom are to read outside your genre as much as possible, some literary works, for example, if you wish to elevate your writing and make your work stands out from the crowd of authors in one genre. Only then will you develop your own voice and style. If your work catches on with an audience, then you will be successful on your own terms and not as an also-ran.

Fred G. Baker is a hydrologist, historian, and writer living in Colorado. He writes fiction and non-fiction books and articles. He specializes in science fiction/fantasy, mystery/espionage, and thrillers. He is the author of An Imperfect Crime, Desert Sanctuary, Desert Underworld, Einstein's Raven, Zona: The Forbidden Land, Life, Death, and Espionage, The Black Freighter, and the Modern Pirate Series of short and long stories. For more information, please see his website: othervoicespress.com.

Never Give Up

Written by Michael O. Borthwick

I never set out to write a book; it just happened. In December 2019, I became ill and never fully recovered, even to this day. Before I got sick, I was an avid bicycle rider averaging over 5,600 miles a year, with a few races in the mix. I found myself no longer able to ride with time on my hands. At the same time, I heard about someone else going through serious health issues, and I wanted to share with them what comforted me during life's challenges; my relationship with God.

After giving a short summary of how I came to have a personal relationship with God to the one facing health issues, I took a more in-depth look at who 'The God of the Bible' would clarify why a personal relationship with God is needed. This led to the writing of 'A Mechanic's Handbook To The God Of The Bible.'

Just as the Bible doesn't edit out the failures of its Saints, I didn't edit out my failures, clearly showing how a loving God became my source of strength and peace, especially during challenging times.

The long-lasting effects of the earlier illness create extreme fatigue and brain fog, making it hard to concentrate and impossible to work a full day. At home, though, sitting at my computer, I could focus and write for hours on end—a true miracle.

Writing and self-publishing my story in a book is outside my comfort zone, so I am glad the experience of sharing my story has been incredibly positive and rewarding. The promotion side of the book was made easier through using the OnlineBookclub BOTD, another positive experience.

Michael O. Borthwick is a business owner, automotive mechanic, and author of the book 'A Mechanic's Handbook To The God Of The Bible / Why God Just Makes Sense'. The book received excellent reviews from Onlinebookclub. In his early years, his passion was racing motorcycles, cars and dirt bikes. Mike writes about how he came to have a relationship with 'the God of the Bible' through near-death experiences in his early twenties. Mike's relationship with God spans over 40 years and is still strong. Mike has four children and four grandchildren and lives in Canada with his wife, Kathy.

Confessions of a Writer

Written by N. L. Holmes

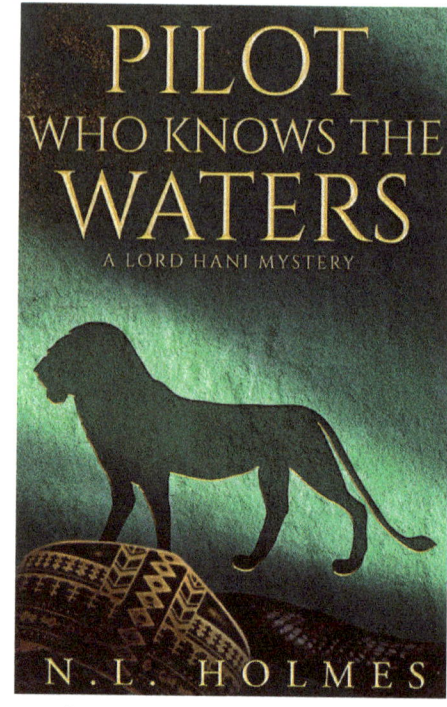

Shortly before I retired from teaching, I decided many historical events in the deep past were interesting enough to cry out for a fictionalized treatment. I have read all my life voraciously (and that's the best training for writing). Still, at that point, I began to study the craft of writing—reading books on the subject, attending conferences, and participating in a writers' group. The most valuable thing I did was complete a manuscript and send it to a professional editor for critique. This is worth all the books on the writer's craft you can buy because it's very concrete. My most extensive advice is to invest in professional editing, no matter how many books you have. And this is especially important for independent authors, who may not have any other quality control.

Then came the querying of an agent. Perseverance is the name of the game. It will undoubtedly take months and maybe years. I happened upon one almost accidentally, and she was negotiating with a publisher. But we eventually parted ways over an issue of artistic conscience. I didn't even realize it was important to me until it came up. Then I confronted a choice.

If I went for traditional publication again, I had the long querying process ahead; then the agent would have to shop each of my by-then seven or eight books. Then a publisher would only put them out once per year at most. In short, I would be pretty old before I ever got started! I decided to publish independently instead, which has worked well for me.

Since then, I have also published traditionally, and I can compare the two. Publicity is the most challenging part—writers are not self-promoters by nature. But even a small publisher will make you do much of your own publicity. Going indie is much work with a steep learning curve, and I've made some really embarrassing mistakes! But you retain control over every step if that's important to you.

N.L. Holmes is the pen name of a professional archaeologist who received her doctorate from Bryn Mawr College. She has excavated in Greece and Israel and taught ancient history and humanities at the university level for many years. She has always had a passion for books, and in childhood, she and her cousin (also a writer today) used to write stories for fun.

To All the Naysayers

Written by J. E. Hibpshman

I was born with a learning disability, and at age 10, a teacher told me I was too stupid to read. I decided that day to write a book to prove her wrong. One day I decided I had better get moving, or I would not prove that teacher wrong. I finally sat down and started writing my book. Honestly, I did not have the story outlined; I just started writing. I wanted the people to act like I have seen people act: strong, willful, deceitful, courageous, violent, and so forth. The book developed from there. In the end, I self-published through Book Baby.

I was surprised that I started writing the book to check off a life box, but the more I wrote, the more I enjoyed the process and, frankly, the more fun I had doing it. I know many have said it's hard work, and at times, it is hard, but I enjoyed the ride from beginning to end. I find my mind wanders while writing, and I just let the story follow along. Sometimes I'm surprised by what happens.

Like everyone, I enjoy good reviews, but I write for myself.

Most of my online reviews have been good, but a few people said they did not like the book. To me, that's okay. No book is for everyone. I want to learn what I can from negative reviews and then let it go. I allow no one to live rent-free in my head.

J. E. Hibpshman lives in Palmer, Alaska, with his wife of 40 years. He spent time in the Marine Corps in construction and law enforcement. He took those experiences and put them into the people in his books. Hibpshman learned to read as an adult and now enjoys reading. He has discovered that writing brings him even more joy. He spends his days now working, writing, and enjoying the family.

The Agents-That-Weren't

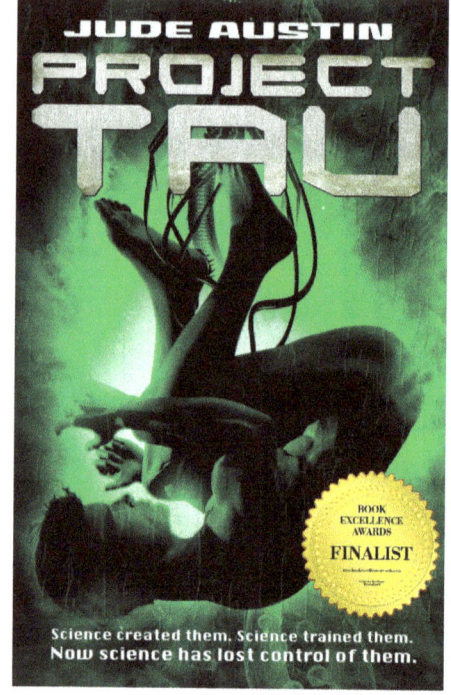

Written by Jude Austin

Since I completed my first (still unpublished) novel and dove into publishing at the tender age of eighteen, I've had four literary agents represent me. Wait. That sounds far too impressive. A more accurate description would be, "I fell into four huge phony-agent traps that I wish I'd known about earlier, and now I'm writing this article to help someone avoid those same mistakes."

So, without further ado, the saga of the agents!

The first agent I signed with tried to make me sign with a vanity publisher. I wasn't sure why this agent was pushing me to sign with these people and hand over a commission when vanity publishers take more or less everyone who comes along, agented or not.

The second actually did some agent-like things, such as approaching Dimension Films to discuss the novelization rights for a movie I wanted. Unfortunately, they charged me $150 per month for "running costs." Seriously, any agency relying on their clients to pay the electric bill before they even make a sale isn't worth the time.

The third did neither of those things, and I was with them for about three years. Unfortunately, they did nothing else.

It wasn't until I inadvertently read an article on an acquisition editor's blog about them being blacklisted from most traditional publishers due to mass spamming that I could do much better. I also got confirmation of the mass spamming when I was accidentally included in one of Agent 3's emails, so we parted company on amicable terms.

The final one tried to get me to pay in-house editors to look at the manuscript. They then said it would take much work to fix it after I'd received a glowing report from the editor in question.

At this point, I gave up and went to Amazon KDP. The good news is that anyone can publish their work there.

Jude has been writing for several years and is the author of the multi-award-winning Projects series. She lives in Japan, where she alternates between gaming, working on her next book and binge-watching Netflix.

Her genre is sci-fi realism, AKA character-driven, non-dystopian sci-fi without the advanced science, aliens, AI/robots or epic space battles, as she prefers creating other worlds and cultures.

You can subscribe to her newsletter at https://www.judeaustin.net

How I Became a Writer

Written by Michael J. Bowen

I grew up wanting to be a professional tennis player. Fast-forward to November 1985, I was a senior in college playing tennis at UNC-Wilmington. The city of Wilmington, dubbed "Hollywood East," was home to Screen Gem Studios. On a brisk November day, two talent agents from the studio approached me at the university student union. They were looking for extras to play in an upcoming Arnold Schwarzenegger movie. The following morning, I showed up for my acting debut and a few seconds of fame. It was a day that changed my life forever. After filming, I drove off the movie set and stopped at a busy intersection. With the coast seemly clear, I pressed the gas pedal. I never saw the oncoming car that hit my driver's side door, instantly paralyzing me from the neck.

My book, The Viewfinder, recounts that fateful day and what happened to me in the days that followed. The title came to me during the final rewrite. When describing the vibrant images I saw while languishing in my mangled car, I was reminded of pictures you see through a toy viewfinder.

I became a writer to tell my story in my own words. I wanted the reader to feel the roller-coaster ride of emotions I experienced during this pivotal time in my life and to understand the life lessons I learned.

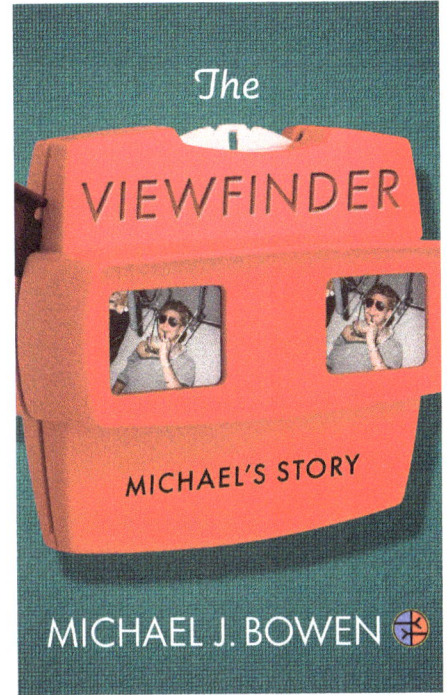

One surprising thing I learned about creating a successful book is that timing your book's promotion and launch date is critical to its success. That said, a successful promotion will bring more good and bad reviews. For my health, staying even-keeled is important, so I rarely read reviews.

Michael J. Bowen grew up in Washington Park, North Carolina, waterskiing on the glassy water of the Tar River and playing competitive sports. On November 19, 1985, as a college senior, he made the fateful decision to play an extra in an Arnold Schwarzenegger movie. That decision led to a car accident, paralysis, and a spiritual intervention to teach me lessons about faith, empathy, and overcoming adversity. Today he is a "walking" quadriplegic, retired physed teacher, high school tennis coach, and motivational speaker. A confessed beach bum and amateur drummer.

My Publishing Journey

Written by Peter S. Rush

Dreaming of being a writer is a long way from actually being one. When I seriously considered writing a profession, my first challenge was making a living. I thought I would write a best-selling novel and be on my way. I wrote the novel and got an agent in New York. I have a nice folder of rejection letters from publishers. Two years of wasted effort. I turned to journalism and found a job working for a trade magazine. After getting married, life took over. I did learn that to be a writer, you need to write. I never lost the desire to write the novel. Several years ago, a story that had been turning around in my mind for years found its way onto paper. With fits and starts, I wrote a first draft and a second draft – found an editor to be brutally honest with me. I wrote another draft, and then another one, and another one after that.

I relearned the craft of writing, character development, and moving a plot to a climax. It was an incredible journey. Finally, it was done, but publishers were nowhere to be found. I went the independent route, as most writers must do today. I was a bit disappointed not to find a publisher.

However, I learned a great deal about the publishing industry. The most important lesson was to write a quality book. I submitted my novel to some contests and was awarded first prize in several of them.

I've also joined a writer's group that allowed me to meet some great people. I am grateful that the effort was well received. Can I make a living off the proceeds – not yet? Perseverance does pay off. My second novel was published during the pandemic, and the marketing had begun.

There are so many layers to being a successful writer. I'm working on a third. Writing doesn't get easier, but the reward is there if you remain confident in your story.

Peter S. Rush is a graduate of Brown University and has a Master's in Creative Writing from the University of Florida. He was a newspaper reporter, magazine editor, Peace Corps volunteer, and police officer. He was the CEO of a global management company. His first novel Wild World received the Independent Press Award for New Fiction (Debut), the National Indie Excellence Award for New Adult Fiction, and two Beverly Hills Book Awards in Social/Political Change and Regional Fiction Northeast.

The Greatest Gift

Written by Rob White

As I honed my writing skills and developed my unique style, I found I had access to something truly powerful. It's the greatest gift that writing has given me. I call it Influential languaging.

As I sharpened my writing manner, my self-talk began taking on a cutting edge. I could now language my thoughts into dynamic, new patterns that influenced my daily way of thinking about things. It was no longer the same old, everyday, usual stuff.

This new way of thinking had me pondering my future with eager curiosity. My new adeptness in languaging was affecting every aspect of my life. It helped me reshape the way I was being in the world, which gave a new shape and form to my world.

Furthermore, it was only after I began writing that it occurred to me how my experiences in the world were always a product of the language I used to talk to myself about what was happening. Before this, I always thought my circumstances gave me my experiences, and subsequently, they gave me my mood and attitude.

Wow, now I realized that by the time I'd had my morning coffee and brushed my teeth, my style of self-talk had already determined my mood for the day.

And if I deliberately languaged my thoughts in a sharp and uplifting way: I was "already an optimist" before my day came into play.

However, if my languaging was dull and downtrodden: I was "already a pessimist" just waiting to happen. That was mind-boggling.

At this juncture, my writing took on a whole new purpose. I deliberately began using my new languaging skills to write a great book and design an inner monologue that gave me the life I dreamed of living.

Rob White, born into a conversation, in an impoverished small mill town, fraught with thoughts of lack and limit, was always in trouble. One day, after mocking the school principal, White was called into the office and offered an incredible piece of advice.

The principal paused and said, "Bobby... your world will always occur to you as troubling. That's because you're a troublemaker, always waiting to happen. Your world won't change unless you do."

White was stunned. He'd never heard anything like that before. Over the next seven decades, this message lifted him to many dimensions of higher living.

The Greatest Gift

Written by Van Fleisher

I would have laughed at the thought of sharing any words of wisdom concerning writing or publishing a few years ago. Equally, I would have felt comfortable talking about marketing. Now that I have written and published three books, I realize that my fear and comfort were juxtaposed.

Writing a book is simply storytelling. It can be a real story, an imagined one, or a hybrid. You have to get the words on a file or paper, and you can get help from a grammar app. You'll probably also need an editor. Or, you could be an amazing storyteller with a good voice and a recording set-up so that you could submit audio files.

Technology is so simple and comprehensive that with some artwork for a cover, along with a digital manuscript, a book can be published in 15 minutes. Seriously. But that's the easy part.

Marketing is a black art combined with algorithms. In my experience, I've spent more money on marketing training than on marketing. There is an entire industry of people, companies, and apps that will "make you a best seller!" The most important two words of wisdom are "buyer beware."

Another piece of advice is not to trust your friends for objective feedback.

They value your friendship more than advising that they may not be qualified to give.

If it's your first time publishing, consider a hybrid like BookBaby. They'll help get your book out and help with the ebook formatting, which you'll need unless you're a programmer.

And finally, write to have fun because it's tough to make a living.

During my first two careers – one with an airline and the other in management consulting- Van lived on planes and in airports. The only healthy antidote to the terminal and in-flight boredom was reading, so he read every thriller in the airport bookstores.

Van retired at age 73, and when he woke up on his first retirement day, he didn't know what to do. So, he figured that if Clancy and Patterson could do it, so could he.

Donny and Mary Grace's California Adventures

Catherine A. Pepe

The ten-year-old Mary Grace Miller and her family—her brother, Donny, and her father and mother, Mr. and Mrs. Miller, respectively—always had a nice time together in Wichita, Kansas. They would severally visit the Sedgwick County Zoo together to see the animals, especially the penguins, which Donny loved seeing and playing with. They also had a wonderful home provided by the church and could do lunch-out picnics and go swimming together.

All that changed when Mr. and Mrs. Miller were sent to missionary work in Kenya, a country in Africa, by the St. James Episcopal Church. Mary Grace and Donny were very upset that they would have to go to California to stay with their grandparents for the two years their parents would be away. Little did they know there was so much to encounter.

I loved every story in this book—especially the encounters both Mary Grace and Donny had in California. It was wonderful reading about how the Millers always had fun as a family, and I loved seeing their unique bond and love for each other. They all treated Donny, who had Down's Syndrome, with love and care. After going to California, I enjoyed the cocktail of events the duo (Mary and Donny) went through. They had both good times and bad times.

The book handles the case of how detrimental parents' behaviors can be to their children. After losing his grandmother, Jason must have felt very hurt. His father, inconsiderate of his actions and how they hurt other people, only worsened Jason. Jason would find it normal to bully other students, and he didn't see using hurtful words against others as a thing. However, I am pleased with how well the teachers handled his case and made him a better boy—a testimony that anyone can change if shown the right direction. Jason even began being friends with Donny, the person he had been bullying and demeaning.

There's a lot to take from this book. We learn about how children interact, how to treat a child with special needs, being positive like Donny, and the negatives of bullying, among others. I rate this book a 4 out of 4 stars. I recommend this book to children of eight years and above who like novels with mystery.

by official OnlineBookClub Reviewers

The Prodigy Slave, Book One: Journey to Winter Garden

Londyn Skye

The Prodigy Slave, Book One: Journey to Winter Garden, is a historical romance novel by Londyn Skye. It's a story that disturbs the soul and kindles one's imagination to an era when owing an enslaved person to a privileged honorable family is considered normal. The book has twenty-three chapters. Lily, a nine-year-old girl, was forcefully taken from her mother (Maya) to be sold into slavery at a Negro auction by a man she got to know was her father on the same day.

To escape her loneliness, she found solace in teaching herself to play her new master's piano for fourteen years. She was discovered by her master's son (James), who became her childhood friend. However, a turn of events separated and destroyed their friendship for many years. When James returned from medical school, he convinced his father (Jesse Adams) and took her to Ohio to be punished, unknowing of Lily what awaits her.

I rate the book 4 out of 4 stars because it is highly informative and well-researched. No historical romance fiction has ever had me absorbed as much as this book. I must commend the author for creating an intensely character-driven story.

The story is dotted with twists and turns that are filled with suspense. As the story unfolded, the unexpected turns had me glued to the pages. I love everything about this book. There is nothing I dislike about it. Readers can picture what it feels like to be dehumanized, unaccepted, and unwanted. The heartfelt conversation between Lily and James reminded me of my past relationship. Landon is my favorite character. I admire the fact that he is humorous and intelligent. Also, his excellent managerial skills fueled Lily's career.

In conclusion, I recommend this book to people who think racism is a myth or overrated. Also, people who like historical and romance novels will enjoy this book.

by official OnlineBookClub Reviewers

Natural Relief for Anxiety and Stress: A Practical Guide

Gustavo Kinrys, MD
Alexandra Gold, M.A.

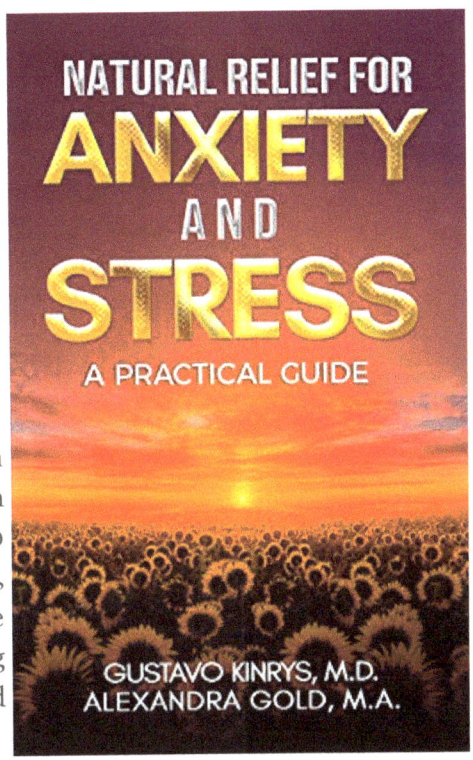

According to the Anxiety and Depression Association of America, anxiety disorders are the most common mental illness in the United States. With over 40 million adults affected by the highly treatable disorder, it is surprising to learn that only 36.9% receive treatment. As I thought about these staggering statistics, I realized that a majority of those affected may be against treatment because they don't want to rely on daily medication or have to deal with inconvenient side effects, which is where Natural Relief for Anxiety and Stress: A Practical Guide comes in. Gustavo Kinrys, M.D., and Alexandra Gold, M.A., have developed a guide for patients with anxiety and stress. Their self-help guide is a quick reference read that specifies certain vitamins, herbs, and nutrients that can be beneficial to treat ailments. At right at 150 Kindle edition pages, I found the book to be a light, easy read. Along with introducing specific foods, there is mention of special exercises and meditations that can give peace to the mind and project the appropriate amount of serotonin.

The book was exceptionally well-edited, and I found no errors. While reading, my favorite thing is that the two writers noted foods with the necessary vitamins, herbs, and minerals, meaning several items I already had in my home to try. I also admired that they designated which foods and nutrients would help with which ailments, giving readers particular items to try to see results.

Natural Relief for Anxiety and Stress: A Practical Guide is an appropriate read for anyone interested in managing anxiety and stress. The language is professional and direct, yet easy to understand, and the instructions and tips seem easy to follow while reading.

I thoroughly enjoyed reading Natural Relief for Anxiety and Stress: A Practical Guide and am happy to rate it 4 out of 4 stars. This book received a high rating mainly due to how the information was presented. The treatments were organized to correlate with ailments, making the book easily classified as a quick reference guide. This is the type of book that is nice to keep around and refer back to when you're looking for some specific remedies. I recommend this book to anyone seeking healthy coping mechanisms for anxiety and stress while being able to refrain from conventional medications.

by official OnlineBookClub Reviewers

Preppers Medical Handbook

William W. Forgey, M.D.

THE PREPPER'S
MEDICAL
HANDBOOK

How to provide medical care when
you can't rely on anyone but yourself

WILLIAM W. FORGEY, M.D.

Have you ever lost a loved one to an emergency health breakdown because you didn't know what to do? Have you suffered deterioration in health due to a delay in getting medical help? If you've experienced either of these, Preppers Medical Handbook by William Forgey may have been a lifesaver. However, you should still have a copy handy for other emergencies that might arise in the future.

This book takes first-aid to a whole new paradigm. It provides a step-by-step guide on handling emergency health challenges if help is either not coming or will take a while. The author takes the time to show the reader how to handle various health conditions — from body malfunction to organ dysfunction. He delves into off-grid assessment and treatment of common diseases and health conditions. There are a plethora of solutions to different health challenges this handbook covers. I highly recommend that everyone should get a copy of this book.

I was endeared to this book because it opened my eyes to things I should have known.

What I liked most was the format and arrangement of the book. The author was thoughtful enough to know that readers might be interested in different aspects of this book. To that end, he hyperlinked texts connecting the reader to detailed resources on a particular subject. For instance, when he talked about how pulmonary embolus can mimic pneumonia, there was a link to more detailed information about pneumonia. Hence, if the reader needed more information about pneumonia, it could be easily and quickly accessed. Thus, navigating through different topics in this book was seamless.

The book's first chapter laid the foundation for the reader to benefit from its content. The author laid out four ways this book should be read. This outline gave me an idea of what to expect from the book. Also, it showed that this book shouldn't be a one-time read — it should be a resource to refer to continually.

The author also used diagrams to show how some steps in the book should be followed. This would help the untrained reader to apply these steps as though they had been trained.

Everything about this book was top-notch — the writing, editing, and delivery. I rate it 4 out of 4 stars. People who live in remote areas, where access to a health facility could take much time, should have this book handy. I also recommend it to everyone.

by official OnlineBookClub Reviewers

The Biblical Clock: The Untold Secrets Linking the Universe and Humanity with God's Plan

Daniel Friedmann
Dania Sheldon

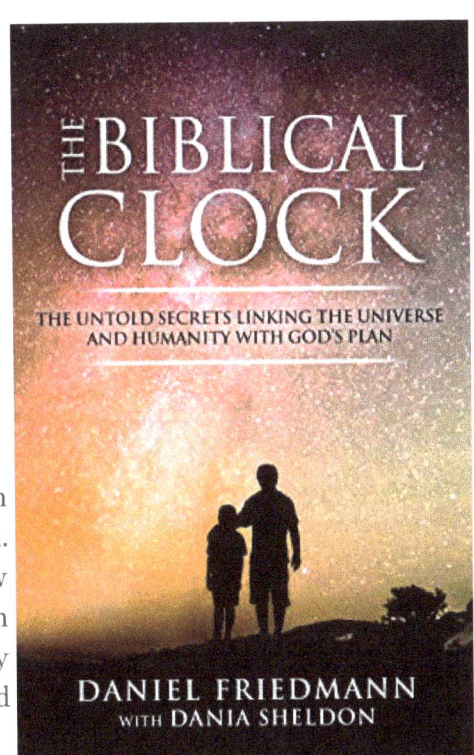

One of the debates that still rages on in our time with no sign of ending soon is creation versus evolution. What do you know about Simon Bar Kokhba? How different is the Messiah ben Joseph from the Messiah ben David? How can the repeated patterns of history based on the established spiritual year cycles be used to predict the events during the End of Days?

In the beginning, we find Isaac ben Samuel in Acre, a town besieged by the Mamluks. Acre is about to fall, but this exceptional Kabbalist will be spared and taken captive. As the book progresses, his significance becomes more apparent. The book is packed with fascinating conversations, enacted historical dialogues, and remarkable figures, including Kabbalists, world leaders, and other characters that many may not have heard about them. Apart from the universe's age, there are discussions on themes such as free will.

It is exciting to see that there is a wealth of information that could help reconcile one of the biggest debates on the planet. More importantly, it is not just about pitting religion and science against each other but also showing that the two corroborate. Many will be surprised, as I was, that several centuries ago, many rabbis began making calculations way ahead of science; with a few adjustments, the ages they found to fall within the range of the current scientific estimates. One of the most incredible aspects of the book is, therefore, making that which would be inaccessible to many easily accessible. With such a resource in your library, you can be rest assured that you will learn much more and be prepared to give answers defending both science and your faith; it is not one or the other anymore. I also enjoyed how the author presented his arguments by combining dialogues, stories, and visual presentations like tables, making the book suitable for everyone.

I have read a few books that dared to solve the apparent conflict between evolution, creation, and the age of the Earth, but none provided a solid answer. In the end, they were arguing for the claims of one against the other. I rate it 4 out of 4 stars. The book is suitable for anyone puzzled by the apparent discrepancies between science and religion on the origin and age of the universe.

by official OnlineBookClub Reviewers

The Smartest Person in the Room: The Root Cause and New Solution for Cybersecurity

Christian Espinosa

Business owners depend on their cybersecurity team to keep their corporate data secure. Author Christian Espinosa contends that these technical professionals cause the issue in his book The Smartest Person in the Room. Data theft is caused by people and their poor communication skills, not by a lack of cutting-edge technology. People's urge to be the smartest person in the room and poor people skills prevent them from effectively communicating with others to solve problems is the main reason we are losing the cybersecurity war. The author demonstrates how to raise employee empathy levels, alter their perspectives, and improve general awareness.

This book is primarily intended for those engaged in the cyber war today. However, technical professionals attempting to advance their careers might also find this book helpful. The book imparts the core methods, people skills, and life skills necessary to excel in any line of work.

The author has discussed ways to increase awareness, alter mindset, improve communication, and practice Kaizen. He also discusses techniques for meditation that can aid in cultivating a winning attitude. Espinosa has provided examples from his own life to support his arguments.

The book has been expertly edited. Its wording is straightforward to understand. The book is appropriate for non-technical people because the author doesn't use complicated or technical phrases. It discusses exercises for developing a winning mindset, and the author advises readers to perform them diligently. I liked these activities, and as a manager, I've highlighted a few I would do with my staff.

I rate the book 4 out of 4 stars. I highly recommend it to all employers and those looking to advance their careers. You do not need to be in the business of cybersecurity to read this book. The book is suitable for those who want to improve their people skills and professional lives.

The Unfakeable Code®: Take Back Control, Lead Authentically and Live Freely on Your Terms

Tony Jeton Selimi

Created from a combination of decades of research in philosophy, metaphysics, biology, theology, mathematics, and engineering, Tony Jeton Selimi's The Unfakeable Code® presents a detailed guide to discovering your authentic self and living your best life. Many of us have low-level thinking problems, masks that develop our transient one-sided personas, and harmonize our inner demons and angels.

However, as the book title suggests, we are introduced to five "mind-upgrading, life-enhancing, and business-transforming" principles (from unmasking and knowing our true selves to gain a deep understanding of love).

I have to say that I found this guide helpful in many ways, especially in developing a deeper awareness of myself. Showing similarities between the code of the human mind and the code of a computer program, including the need to upgrade this code constantly, the author opts for a logical approach, presenting readers with his lessons through numerous instances they can easily relate to. From the different ways we engage in self-deceit to people-pleasing, Tony Jeton Selimi covers a lot of what it means to live a fake life with our masks while even employing his personal stories and experiences with his clients to illustrate what it means to come into your authentic self finally.

I was also drawn to how the author consistently encouraged viewing yourself and others from a non-judgmental perspective. He acknowledges that you are not perfect and consist of good and evil, but it is important to find a balance.

Overall, The Unfakeable Code® is a unique, highly beneficial guide that will help many readers on their journey toward personal and professional development. Readers can also look forward to the ten Behavioural Change Principles® (BCP®) included, which will serve to change their mentalities. Applying the lessons requires much effort on the reader's part. Therefore, if you are willing to put in the work and are interested in self-development and becoming one with your unfakeable self, then you will massively benefit from the contents of this book. I rate this guide 3 out of 4 stars.

by official OnlineBookClub Reviewers

Timewise

Robert Leet

I rarely come across books that cut across diverse topics. Timewise by Robert Leet is an example of such a book. It is also highly educative and contains an exciting sci-fi story blended with romance.

Ron Larsen, a fictional character in the book, narrates the story. Ron had an unstable childhood upbringing. He was an orphan who was bounced around several foster homes, making it hard to maintain a stable relationship or create worthwhile memories. Ron's story took a turn when he met Regina Russo, a beautiful female physics professor. Although Ron had several relationships with other women, his relationship with Regina is special. To Ron, Regina is his mentor and friend he fell in love with when he was 14. So, when she came to him with a seemingly dangerous but intriguing scientific project, he had no choice but to oblige. Read to discover the mind-blowing innovations Regina and Ron intend to use to change the future.

The book was riddled with several scientific concepts, especially physics, and mathematics. It also contained diagrams, which were very helpful in explaining some scientific concepts. The storyline is very captivating. I love the way the author created the idea of predicting the future. The concept of using mathematical calculations and physics laws to predict the future made the storyline unique with a real-life setting. The romantic nature of the book also made the book more compelling. I love the analogy behind the ending part of the book and Ron's beginning. Also, Ron's conversation with Diana Fletcher when they were playing chess almost mirrors his encounter with Regina years ago.

The book also had excellent character and scene development. The characters (major and minor) were well-developed, with their roles clearly expressed. The characters were also able to convey emotions.

In terms of grammatical errors, the book is flawless. The author was also able to articulate his thoughts and ideas properly. Therefore, I am rating this book 4 out of 4 stars. I recommend this book to sci-fi lovers, especially those interested in stories revolving around quantum physics.

by official OnlineBookClub Reviewers

We are Voulhire: A New Arrival under Great Skies

Matthew Tysz

Galen became his uncle's heir to the Onita Steel business. He was traveling to the Land of the Princes in Magnum Caelum, a part of the Voulhirian Kingdom under the Government of King Wilhelm. In the Hillport countryside above Magnum Caelum, Lord Eldus Alderman, a former judge, was appointed by the king in this economically declined place. If Galen was starting to learn the forge in Magnum Caelum, Lord Eldus would also investigate the anomaly of the previous management. One day, Lord Eldus was confused while receiving unusual stones from an unknown sender. Was it a sign of a bad omen? Abruptly, dancing soldiers were coming. Why? On the other hand, Galen and Rowan (his guide) noticed a mage on the mining site while looking for "lactis" upon his request. They investigated as well as found rare stones. Were these similar to Lord Eldus's stones? If you're looking for an enthralling science-fiction book, try to read the first book of this series written by Matthew Tysz, We are Voulhire: A New Arrival under Great Skies. I recommend this book to anyone fond of reading this genre, and anybody who likes political thrillers will also enjoy the cryptic political twists of the author's creative writing style.

One of Matthew's strengths in weaving this tale is the foundation of the plot. He laid out strong character development, albeit a bit slowly. The author is wittingly gifted when to add or end the supporting characters. The twists and turns are quite shocking. I will rate We are Voulhire: A New Arrival under Great Skies 4 out of 4 stars.

by official OnlineBookClub Reviewers

Wilderness Cry: A Scientific and Philosophical Approach to Understanding God and the Universe

Hilary L. Hunt M.D.

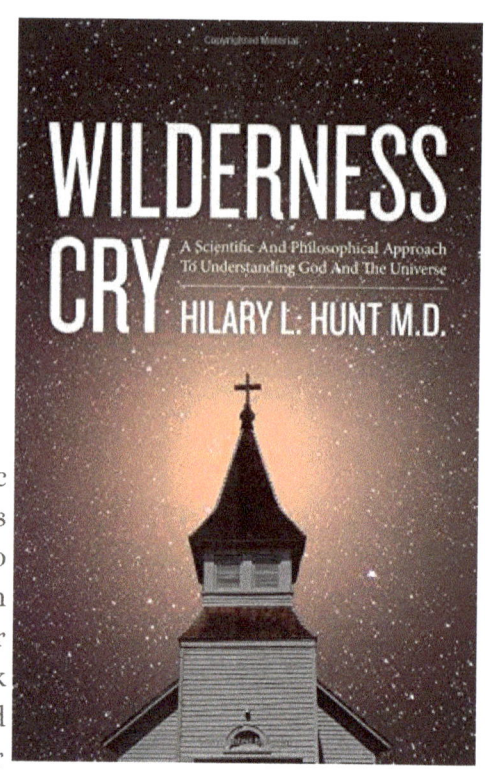

Wilderness Cry by Hilary L Hunt, M.D. is a scientific and philosophical inquiry into Bible teachings compared to denominational teachings. It attempts to provide logic through reason of the common assumptions Christians have, most of which are either due to ignorance or illogical beliefs. The book interrogates the motivation of early Bible writers and their attempt to force people into believing that their actions may or may not affect their destiny.

Hilary believes that God's perfection renders Him assertive, and He, therefore, is not vulnerable enough to be influenced by either man's positive or negative actions. The author discusses various inconsistencies in church doctrines; for example, in the past, priests presided over mass with their backs to the congregation, while in contemporary times, they faced the congregation. In addition, Hilary questions the assumption that only rational beings (humans) will go to heaven and animals (irrational) cannot because they cannot communicate with God. He also argues that there is a possibility of the Jordan meeting between Jesus and John being staged, as it's not logical for cousins living in the same vicinity not to have met to discuss their different views on the Jewish religion.

I believe this book merits a rating of 4 out of 4 stars for its boldness and clarity in addressing Christian issues. What I liked most was the author's ability to justify the title's relevance in his discussions. He paints a picture of one who innocently thirsts for knowledge and graphically represents the current religious state of Christians as those who hunger for the truth after centuries of misinformation. I also loved his simplistic approach to deconstructing the trinity, and his explanation was far easier to understand.

The book is professionally edited and does not contain a single grammatical error. I recommend it to readers who wish to engage in religious debates and are open-minded enough not to be offended by some contradictions or defiance portrayed by the author.

AUTHOR INTERVIEW

Strong Heart

Charlie Sheldon

When did you first realize you wanted to be a writer?

When I was eight years old.

How do you schedule your life when you are writing?

I write daily, usually in the mornings, although this is not sacrosanct. What is sacrosanct is working daily when writing a story, usually after years of thinking, research, and pondering.

What would you say is your interesting writing quirk?

I am a binge writer, meaning when I write a novel, I work every single day, sometimes for hours at a time, to keep the thread of the story alive and real, but then there are periods of months and years devoted to research as well. And then sometimes are entirely fallow, idle, resting. In 50 years of writing novels, I have finished 9 and rewritten several of them many times, which comes to one book every 5 years. This last series I have done is the best I could do, I am happy with it, and that feels good.

How did you get your book published?

I met someone starting a new publishing company, IronTwine Press, and gave him rough drafts of all three books in the series in late 2015, just before I shipped out for six months on a ship. When I returned, he told me he wanted to publish the series, and he has done so.

Where did you get your information or idea for your book?

The series rose from a combination of hiking in Olympic National Park on Washington State's Olympic Peninsula, years of working with Puget Sound tribes and realizing all First Peoples have a legend of always being here in North America, always, several years of research into geology, ice ages, genetics, history, and meteorology, and a fascination with the Northwest Pacific coast.

After receiving a Masters in Wildlife Biology from UMass in 1971, Charlie Sheldon became a commercial fisherman in New England. Later he worked for seaports for 28 years. In 2012 he returned to sea with the Sailor's Union of the Pacific, serving four years as Able Bodied Seaman and Bosun.

Always a writer, Charlie began working on ideas for his Strong Heart Series, tales of the Olympic Mountains, the Pacific coast, and human origins long, long ago. These days he hikes in the Olympics, cooks for his wife, and rows his Adirondack guide boat on Puget Sound.

Terms of Service: Subject to Change Without Notice

Craig W. Stanfill

When did you first realize you wanted to be a writer?

I didn't plan to become a writer; it just happened.

I'd been concerned for some time about the erosion of freedom on the internet and how social media companies seem to be monitoring everything we do. This prompted me to sit down at the keyboard and write a couple of pages, imagining what it would be like to live in the world we seem to be creating.

Here is part of what I wrote:

"The AIs are always here, watching everything I do. What do I read? What do I write? What do I hear? What do I say? What makes me happy? What makes me sad? Constantly observing, correlating, and measuring. Can they read my mind? Not precisely, but they can infer a lot. They usually know what I think before I do.

That's when I caught the bug. First, a chapter, then a novel, and now a second with more in the works."

Where did you get your information or idea for your book?

Almost everything in the book is based on my life experience as a Ph.D. computer scientist and software entrepreneur. I have used this background to craft a future civilization dominated by artificial intelligence and information technology; indeed, the societal forces unleashed by recent developments in these areas provided the impetus to write in the first place.

What was one of the most surprising things you learned in creating your book?

I discovered that I was good at creating exciting and memorable characters, everything from brief walk-ons to the major players. The break-through moment was when I wrote a fateful interview between my protagonist and her uber boss. Suddenly, someone called 'the Director' leaped off the page, an influential figure memorable for unabashed cynicism and biting honesty interlaced with blatant falsehoods.

Craig W. Stanfill is a computer scientist, entrepreneur, and writer with deep experience in artificial intelligence and parallel computing. He received his Ph.D. in AI from the University of Maryland in 1983, then went on to conduct ground-breaking work in machine learning at Thinking Machines Corporation. In 1994, he founded Ab Initio Software, designing innovative software for parallel enterprise computing. He has been awarded over eighty patents and embarked on a second career as a dystopian science fiction writer. He recently published The Prophecy of the Heron, the second book in his AI Dystopia series.

Endeavor's Run

Tobin Marks

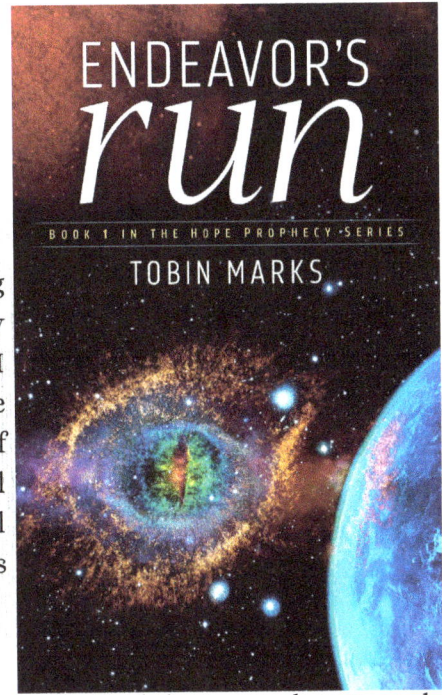

When did you first realize you wanted to be a writer?

I started writing poetry in the early 90s but didn't try writing novels until 2015. However, the story of the Hope Prophecy has been in my head for decades, and I knew that "one day," I would write it. It became an obsession, but I didn't have time to write it down. That all changed in 2015, I found myself with much time on my hands, so I sat down and wrote all three books in about four months. The need for a prequel became evident during the editing process, and it was written in 2017.

How do you schedule your life when you're writing?

I have to schedule writing around my day job. I have an unusual schedule, so much as I work and live at the job site for weeks at a time. While I do get some writing done at work, most of my writing happens when I'm home and can devote both the time and mental state I need to be creative.

What would you say is your interesting writing quirk?

My most interesting writing quirk would probably be the time of day in which I'm most creative. I'm an early-morning writer and love to get up hours before sunrise. This seems to be my most productive time of day. Unless, of course, it's stormy. I love to write with the sound of rain beating down on the roof of my home.

How did you get your book published?

I get most of my research from Google. Like most writers, my search history can be rather odd —things like the effects of nuclear war and dystopian probabilities, to name a couple.

Where did you get your information or idea for your book?

The most surprising thing I discovered when I started writing the Hope Prophecy was that I knew the beginning and the end. Everything in between just sort of evolved as the story went along.

Author Tobin Marks has created an alien watery world called Aqueous. Orbiting a Red Dwarf 1187 light years from Earth, Aqueous is teeming with dangerous reptilian life...and one long-forgotten human colony. Marks is a world traveler who grew up in a household of rocket scientists. As a boy, he had a front-row seat observing many NASA and NOAA projects. Now from his home in northwest Baja, he has written the trilogy: The Hope Prophecy. Book one: Endeavors Run, is a blend of real science, science fiction, and fantasy. Book two: Katana Red, and book three: Drakon Rus, are exciting continuations of the series.

Memoirs of a management consultant - Brief history of my life, professional and other, told by myself

Franco Guazzoni

How did you get your book published?

I had known the publisher NEXO for a while since they had already published a book on my father ("Angelo Guazzoni – the passion for drawing," written by professor Maria Canella) and, more recently, out of commerce, another little book of mine, "Scherzi e versi diversi," a collection of calembours, word puns, and circumstance poetry. So, when NEXO said they were interested in publishing my "Memorie di un consulente di direzione" and later translated it into English, we came very easily to an agreement.

Where did you get your information or idea for your book?

This is an easy question: from my entire life!

As a matter of fact, I had a very eventful life, during which I spent more than fifty years in Management Consulting. I happen to have a strong memory, supported by the many timesheets I had to produce for most weeks of my life, and this helped a lot. Then, practicing my profession, I found that presenting many episodes that happened to me was very interesting for my various audiences. So, with the complicity of COVID, I found the time and the energy to write this book!

What do you like to do when you're not writing?

I take advantage of my old age, thus reading, gardening, traveling a bit, and enjoying my family ... In one word: I live - I do things that in my professional years were not always doable!

How do you process and deal with negative book reviews?

Of course, I am ready to accept them, but they must be well explained. Once, I had one based on wrong assumptions, and I did not like it at all ...

With over 40 years in Management Consulting, Franco Guazzoni has helped over 150 companies of almost all industries think and implement their strategies, improve their financial situations, streamline their operations, and reengineer their processes. Always taking into account the human resources perspective. Thus taking care of change management activities, training, assessment, and coaching. During my career, he has led large groups of Consultants and managers on projects and business teams.

Gateways to Psychotherapy

Michael Hegarty

How do you schedule your life when you're writing?

I take a block of time, say, a week at a time, and do nothing else but writing.

How did you get your book published?

Self-published.

Where did you get your information or idea for your book?

It's taken from my personal life and my therapy work.

What do you like to do when you're not writing?

When I'm not writing or working as a psychotherapist, I paint, fish, and walk, and my sporting passion is attending Rugby Union games.

As a child, what did you want to do when you grew up?

I wanted to be a doctor, specifically, a brain surgeon, but my family had no money available.

Michael was born in Nenagh, Co. Tipperary, and has lived in many counties throughout Ireland. He started his banking career with AIB in Castletownbere, Co. Cork, in 1966. He has resided in Galway since 1981. After a successful career in banking, Michael set up his own financial consultancy practice for private clients at Woodquay, Galway City, in 2001. He also lectured in Family Finance at GMIT to Adult Educational Classes. Michael took Trauma Therapy Training with the World-renowned Trauma and Sensorimotor specialist Janina Fisher. He took courses "Trauma-Informed Stabilisation Treatment" and "Traumatic Attachment & Regulation."
His Mediation training was with Brendan Schutte (Catalyst Consulting) well-known mediator and trainer in the U.K. and Ireland.

After Dark

Noel Hankin

How did you get your book published?

I am a newbie in the vast publishing industry. It was intimidating to me, so I spent many hours researching the rapid changes in the industry and learning about how it works. I decided to hire a company that could walk me through the process. The company I hired is Cascadia, which is in Canada.

Where did you get your information or idea for your book?

I started by drafting the experiences I had and remembered. Then I spent hours interviewing my former partners to gather anecdotes and experiences they had. I then incorporated their input into my draft based on the chronology.

What do you like to do when you're not writing?

I enjoy golf, spending time with my four grandchildren, reading, and traveling.

What was one of the most surprising things you learned in creating your book?

I discovered that, after 50 years, many of us remember certain occasions very differently. For example, I would have sworn that we formed our social club at Clancy's bar. Several of my partners assured me it was Maloney's. All these years, I locked in on an incorrect memory. It made me realize how important it is to write down information before it is forgotten or misremembered. I also noted that some of my partners contradicted each other with specific memories. I had to learn to go with the most reliable source based on my previous experiences with each partner. Some proved to have sharper recollections of details than others.

How do you process and deal with negative book reviews?

It bothered me when my first negative review appeared on Amazon. Then, I read negative reviews about books that won the Pulitzer Prize. Some of the negative comments they received were worse than mine. That made me realize there will always be some people who don't like a particular book.

Noel Hankin is a founder of The Best of Friends, Inc. (TBOF), a pioneering business enterprise that promoted discotheques in New York City starting in 1971. He is the author of After Dark: Birth of the Disco Dance Party, which reveals how TBOF identified a social need in New York City in 1971 and ignited the most important social and cultural happening of the 1970s – the disco boom. Three of their clubs, Leviticus, Justine's, and Bogard's, were among the first black-owned clubs in midtown Manhattan. Hankin is a retired executive who managed some of the world's most valuable consumer brands.

Free And Fearless

Phil Moser

What inspired you to write "Free and Fearless"?

My daughter Brittany was a fascinating and inspiring person. She inspired me to laugh, love, and live in a way I never could imagine. I want to inspire others the same way that I have been inspired.

Was it difficult to write about such an emotional subject?

It was hard to start writing, but it came out beautifully once I started. It came from the bottom of my heart.

What is your next project?

Brittany had a degree in video production to make movies in Hollywood. I want to complete her dream by making a movie about her life story. I have already done one interview. My goal is to inspire others the same way I have been and bring awareness to Addison's disease, with proceeds going to the NADF (National Adrenal Disease Foundation).

How did you create such a special bond with your daughter Brittany?

I loved our two daughters equally. Brittany wanted a close relationship with her parents. She knew her accomplishments were possible only with our support. She was grateful that we spent so much time with her. She loved hearing about our life experiences and wanted to build on them.

Is there anything that you would have done differently?

No, not really. Brittany taught me to be authentic and live in this moment. The kind of love we shared is eternal. As the saying goes, "let's better to love and lose than not loved at all" this could not be more true. Grief is love with no place to go. Brittany understood that and gave us a place to go.

My name is Philip Moser, father of Brittany Moser. I was born in Angola, Indiana, on December 14, 1956. Angola is the county seat of Steuben County, Indiana, located in the very northeastern corner of the state. The county is known for its many lakes and is home to Trine University. I have lived in Steuben County all of my life.

Loss & Discovery

Russell M. Linden

How do you schedule your life when you're writing?

I'm freshest in the morning. I start by responding to important emails, then write for about 2 hours. Take a break, possibly a short walk, and write for another 2-3 hours.

Afternoons are for tasks that don't require heavy thinking – errands, working out, meetings, and the like. Having written several books, I've learned that my brain continually focuses on the book's topics once I start writing. So, I always keep my cell phone or paper/pen with me – at the gym, next to my bed, even when watching a movie/TV. Ideas come when they come, and I'm continually capturing them when they hit me, then processing them later.

How did you get your book published?

I sent my first published book outline and 3 draft chapters. The book was on a "hot" topic, mine was one of the first to address it, and I was fortunate. I worked with the same publisher for the next three books. But ... publishing's become so competitive, and so many publishers are struggling, that my first publisher wouldn't consider this book if I couldn't demonstrate its ability to sell 10,000 copies in the first year. An author I know recently wrote a book for a publisher that doesn't require agents. This publisher works with many religious books, they were interested in my topic, and we made a match.

What was one of the most surprising things you learned in creating your book?

One of the biggest surprises and a true delight was learning that the Torah – written over 2,500 years ago – is as relevant today as it was back then. Rabbi Larry Kushner has captured it well. He says: "The Torah isn't relevant because it happened. It's relevant because it happens."

Russ is a management educator and author of six books. Since the mid-1980s, he has taught executives and managers about leadership and related topics. His latest book is Loss and Discovery: What the Torah Can Teach Us about Leading Change. He has been an adjunct faculty member at the University of Virginia and the Federal Executive Institute since 1985. He has consulted with numerous government agencies, elected officials, and nonprofits in the U.S. and Israel. Russ has advanced degrees from the University of Michigan and the University of Virginia. He and his wife have two adult children and three grandchildren.

UPLIFTED: 12 Minutes to More Joy, Faith, Peace, Kindness & Vitality

Susan Smith Jones

Susan Smith Jones, PhD

When did you first realize you wanted to be a writer?

As an adolescent, I frequently worked as a babysitter with children of all ages. Part of my babysitting accessories was my basket of books I always carried with me so I could read to the children. If any of them ever said to me that they wanted a new book or different and new story time, and I didn't have any extra books with me, I would make up all kinds of stories to tell the children. Each time I would lavishly regale the kids with imaginative, and always positive, stories about young people who were making their dreams come true. Needless to say, I was the most popular and prosperous babysitter in my neighborhood. And it was at this time that I started writing stories about my life and submitted them to magazines. A publishing company read one of my magazine articles and asked me to write a book about my healthy lifestyle. And the rest, they say, is history.

What would you say is your interesting writing quirk?

I make sure my office is tidy and uncluttered when I have a magazine or book assignment with a tight deadline. My mind is always more uplifted and open to ideas and words when I don't have housecleaning chores waiting for me to complete. If I can write outside in nature (backyard, beach, mountains, etc.), I am usually more inspired, and the words flow into my mind more freely.

What do you like to do when you are not writing?

Well, I always enjoy reading books on all topics, and I am always inspired by hiking. I live in both Brentwood (Los Angeles) and England, and when I'm not working, you can usually find me spending lots of time outdoors in nature, which engages the mind without fatigue and yet enlivens it. Charles Darwin, Henry David Thoreau, and Albert Einstein have all written eloquently about the benefits of taking in the natural world.

For decades, Susan has been a renowned leader in holistic health, fitness, human potential, and balanced living. For starters, she taught students/staff/faculty at UCLA how to be healthy and fit for 30 years. Susan travels worldwide as a motivational speaker, consultant, and media talk show guest. She is the author of many health-related books, including her latest Wired for High-Level Wellness and UPLIFTED: 12 Minutes to More Joy, Faith, Peace, Kindness & Vitality.

EDITOR'S PICK

GRACE REVEALED: FINDING GOD'S STRENGTH IN ANY CRISIS BY FREDERICK J. SIEVERT

You can't escape the inevitable crises that will face you throughout your lifetime. Whether it's health problems, emotional issues, career challenges, gut-wrenching losses, or other failures, these experiences can destroy your morale and lead you into deep despair.

In Grace Revealed, you will:

• Enjoy real-life stories of others who discover they are not alone and that relief is within their grasp.

• See how the most devastating afflictions can be overcome through a belief in Jesus and God's unbounded love, mercy, and grace.

• Learn how God's grace transforms lives and will lead you into enduring and rewarding Christian service.

• Be able to encourage others who are suffering but do not have the resources or emotional energy to seek help on their own.

FIRST SURVIVOR BY MARK UNGER

This is a real-life thriller about a family's battle to save their son from a "zero chance of survival" diagnosis. With the world's best doctors and the advocacy of his parents, Louis Unger would fight the battle for his young life. His grit and incredible attitude led to a breakthrough that would change how cancer is treated today. This is not a medical journal or a how-to guide. It is a true page-turner that gives you a front-row seat to a miraculous story of courage, inspiration, and determination. All proceeds from this book will go to the Carrot Seed Foundation, which will fund Neuroblastoma clinical trials and support the children and families stricken by this disease.

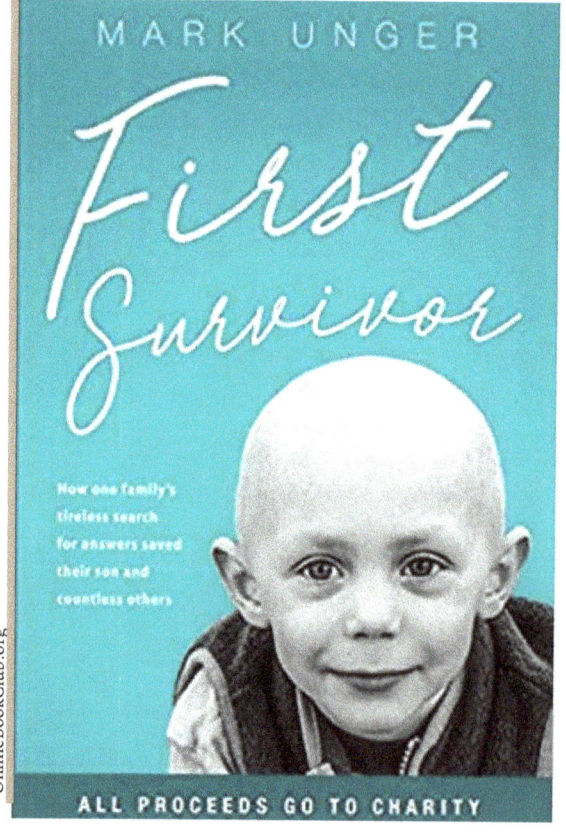